D0288430

1,003
Great Things
About America

Other Books by Lisa Birnbach

1,003 Great Things About Moms
1,003 Great Things About Teachers
1,003 Great Things About Friends
1,003 Great Things About Kids
1,003 Great Things About Getting Older
The Official Preppy Handbook
Lisa Birnbach's College Books
Going to Work
Loose Lips

Other Books by Ann Hodgman

1,003 Great Things About Moms
1,003 Great Things About Teachers
1,003 Great Things About Friends
1,003 Great Things About Kids
1,003 Great Things About Getting Older
My Baby-sitter Is a Vampire (series)
Stinky Stanley (series)
Beat This!
Beat That!

Other Books by Patricia Marx

1,003 Great Things About Moms
1,003 Great Things About Teachers
1,003 Great Things About Friends
1,003 Great Things About Kids
1,003 Great Things About Getting Older
How to Regain Your Virginity
You Can Never Go Wrong by Lying
Blockbuster
Now Everybody Really Hates Me
Now I Will Never Leave the Dinner Table
How to Survive Junior High
Meet My Staff

1,003
Great Things
About America

Lisa Birnbach
Ann Hodgman
Patricia Marx

**Andrews McMeel
Publishing**

Kansas City

1,003 Great Things About America © 2002 by Lisa Birnbach, Ann Hodgman, and Patricia Marx. All rights reserved. Printed in the United States of America. No part of this book may be used or reproduced in any manner whatsoever without written permission except in the case of reprints in the context of reviews. For information, write Andrews McMeel Publishing, an Andrews McMeel Universal company, 4520 Main Street, Kansas City, Missouri 64111.

02 03 04 05 06 BIN 10 9 8 7 6 5 4 3 2 1

Library of Congress Control Card Number 2002105354

Book design and composition by Kelly & Company

——— ATTENTION: SCHOOLS AND BUSINESSES ———

Andrews McMeel books are available at quantity discounts with bulk purchase for educational, business, or sales promotional use. For information, please write to: Special Sales Department, Andrews McMeel Publishing, 4520 Main Street, Kansas City, Missouri 64111.

1,003

Great Things
about America

Our oranges are
much more orange
than foreign oranges.

Cadillacs are still
super-luxurious.

We still own territories.

Frank Lloyd Wright
buildings always
look modern.

All-night
talk-radio shows.

Hawaii is like a
foreign country
that uses our money.

Great
marching bands!

Our judges don't
wear silly wigs.

National
Public Radio.

An SAT coach
on every corner.

Picket fences are
so crisp looking.

You'll always remember
your senior prom, especially
if you weren't invited.

"The thing that impresses me most about America is the way parents obey their children."
—*Edward, Duke of Windsor*

Teen tours.

The bike messenger is a fashion insider.

President William Howard Taft, who weighed 325 pounds, had a bathtub in the White House big enough to hold four men.

Cheerleaders *are* athletes, no matter what anyone says.

(Baton twirlers, maybe not.)

You don't see as many women
in curlers as you used to.

Staying up all night to finish
the homecoming parade float
is a time-honored tradition.

So is not quite getting it
done in time and having to
be in the parade with some
of the chicken wire showing.

Top Ten Names in the U.S.

(Based on Social Security Card Applications for
Births from January Through August 2001)

Boys	Girls
Jacob	Emily
Michael	Hannah
Joshua	Madison
Matthew	Samantha
Andrew	Ashley
Joseph	Sarah
Nicholas	Elizabeth
Anthony	Kayla
Tyler	Alexis
Daniel	Abigail

Alice Waters transformed
American cooking into
American *cuisine*.

With Williams-Sonoma,
The Gap, Banana Republic,
Staples, Toys "R" Us, Starbucks,
7-Eleven, etc., no place in America
feels different from home.

Don't you wish everyone
passed around a peace pipe?

"America is a large, friendly
dog in a very small room.
Every time it wags its tail
it knocks over a chair."
—*Anatole Broyard*

Navajo jewelry.

We're obsessed with
having good breath.
So what's bad about that?

Kansas City has more
fountains than Paris.

Tattoo parlors are now
legal in most states.

Breakfast burritos.

Even someone with a poor credit
rating can buy a car in this country.

We didn't steal the
Elgin Marbles, unlike a
certain country we know.

The surfboard.

People magazine.

FDNY.

I ♥ New York.

The square dance is
the American folk dance
of New Jersey.

"All modern American literature comes from one book by Mark Twain called *Huckleberry Finn*.
—*Ernest Hemingway, 1935*

We have candy shaped like Life Savers and vitamins shaped like Rugrats.

You can buy contact lenses on-line!

We really scared kids
into thinking they had to
wait an hour after eating
before going swimming.

Birthplace
of snowboarding.

Denim shirts look
good on everybody.

Our religious leaders
get into the most
interesting sex scandals!

The Grand Canyon is
100 percent as cool
as everyone says.

Fewer of our baseball players
chew tobacco than they used to.

"O, let America be America again—
The land that never has been yet—
And yet must be."

—*Langston Hughes, 1938*

You can always find a star willing to humiliate him or herself singing the national anthem at the World Series.

The search for the Rockefeller Center Christmas tree takes a full year.

"There's no place like home.
There's no place like home."

Almost no one can
remember Thanksgiving
before Macy's or Labor Day
before Jerry Lewis's telethon.

Other countries don't have
a Miss Subways contest.

Ivory soap is so pure it floats,
although no one knows
why that's such a great thing.

George Washington
was the first person to breed
roses in the United States.

We have the best cactuses.

Curtseying is pretty much over.

Even the District of Columbia
has representatives to Congress.

There's always hope
for Puerto Rico.

"We do not inherit the land,
we borrow it from our children."
—*Native American proverb*

Every southern state
is convinced it makes
the best barbecue.

(And every southern
state is right.)

Robert Frost isn't too hard
to understand, for a poet.

Great American Inventions

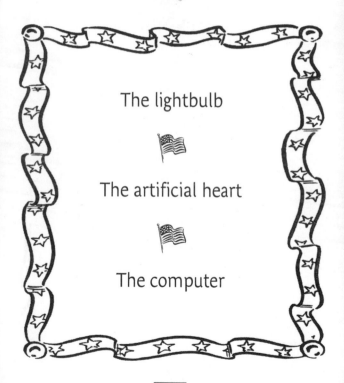

The lightbulb

The artificial heart

The computer

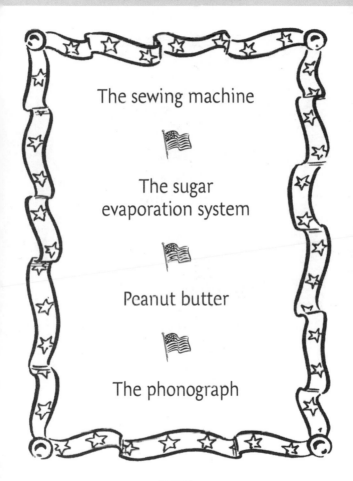

The sewing machine

The sugar
evaporation system

Peanut butter

The phonograph

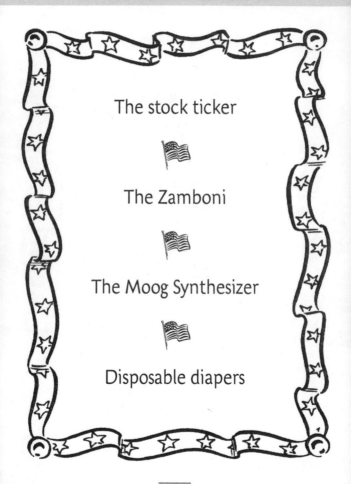

The stock ticker

The Zamboni

The Moog Synthesizer

Disposable diapers

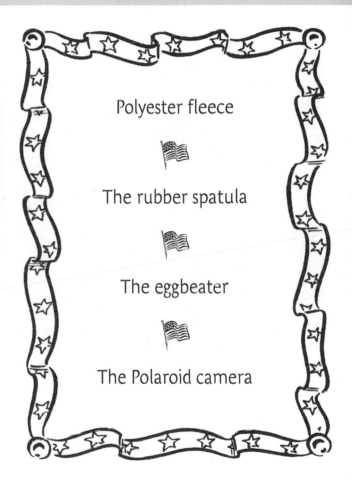

Polyester fleece

The rubber spatula

The eggbeater

The Polaroid camera

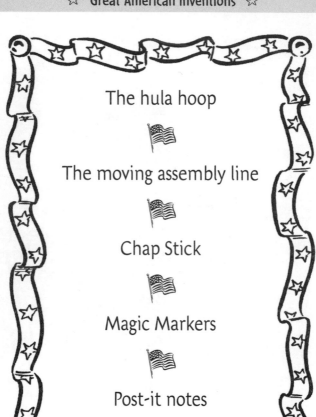

The hula hoop

The moving assembly line

Chap Stick

Magic Markers

Post-it notes

"Eighty percent of married
men cheat in America.
The rest cheat in Europe."

—*Jackie Mason*

The press has the freedom
to print things we are too
tasteful to print here.

The United States would fit into the
continent of Africa 3¼ times, and
yet, we look soooo big on the map.

Street signs are
written in English!

Have you ever seen
more graceful aging than
Kitty Carlisle, Eleanor Powell,
Celeste Holm, or Esther Williams?

We brought popcorn
to the movies.

"Does this boat go
to Europe, France?"
—*Anita Loos*

While he was president,
Ulysses S. Grant was arrested
for exceeding the speed limit
on his horse. He was fined $20.

The horns in most American-made
cars beep in the tone of "F."

Great Obsolete Inventions We're Still Proud Of

The telegraph

The cotton gin

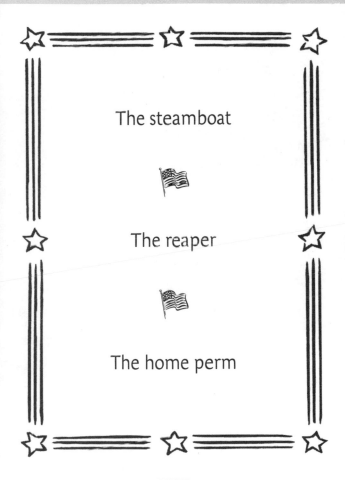

The steamboat

The reaper

The home perm

Alaska is so big that if you
could see a million acres every
day, it would take you a year to
see the entire state.

The state motto of Michigan:
"If you seek a pleasant peninsula,
look about you."

All of our holidays have been
conveniently moved to Monday.

Don't feel like going
to college? Just buy a
diploma through the mail!

We took pizza and
just *ran* with it.

American grandmas
aren't ashamed to wear
tennis skirts to the mall.

When New Coke
was taken off the market,
it made national headlines.

You might not like the song
"Yankee Doodle Dandy," but
try getting it out of your head
once you've heard it.

Get a load of our
amber waves of grain!

Detroit proudly continues to
manufacture cars no one wants.

In Hersheytown, Pennsylvania,
the streetlights are shaped
like Hershey's Kisses.

When Oscar Wilde toured
America, he was a huge hit
in western mining towns.

No one can say American
parents don't get involved
in their children's sports.

Thank God Princess Stephanie's
not an American.

In America, we celebrate the
anniversaries of everything:
when we first met, our first kiss,
the first time we did it, the
first month we made payroll,
our dog's birthday, etc.

TAs who are
just learning English.

Sure the Olympic Committee
may be a teensy bit corrupt, but
we've got the Special Olympics,
and they're just fine.

The divorce rate is not
as high as it used to be.

We smoke less
than Europeans.

A Sno-Kone tastes
the same in Sioux City
as it does in Tallahassee.

". . . is the Seattle of . . ."

Cowboy boots are
great looking even when
you're not on the prairie.

Beware the trendiness
of cowboy hats, however.

Put all the kids in overalls.

Barbie was invented here.

HBO's original series.

Chocolate egg creams.

The concept of sportswear.

"Outside of the killings, [Washington] has one of the lowest crime rates in the country."

—*Marion Barry, [former] mayor of Washington, D.C.*

Home of the quilting bee.

And the spelling bee.

And Bea Benaderet.

Weird Laws Still on the Books

Every citizen in Kentucky is required to take a bath once a year.

In Idaho it is illegal to give someone a box of candy that weighs more than fifty pounds.

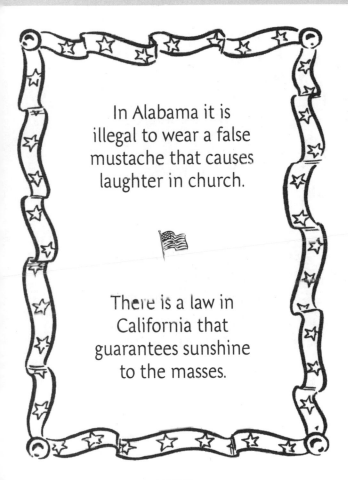

In Alabama it is
illegal to wear a false
mustache that causes
laughter in church.

There is a law in
California that
guarantees sunshine
to the masses.

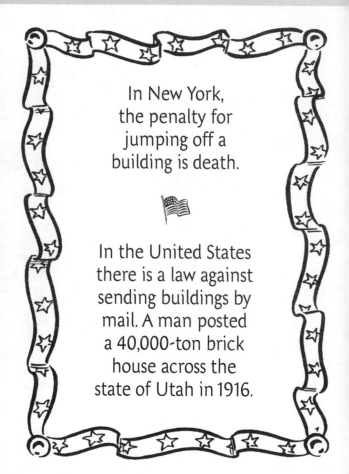

In New York,
the penalty for
jumping off a
building is death.

In the United States
there is a law against
sending buildings by
mail. A man posted
a 40,000-ton brick
house across the
state of Utah in 1916.

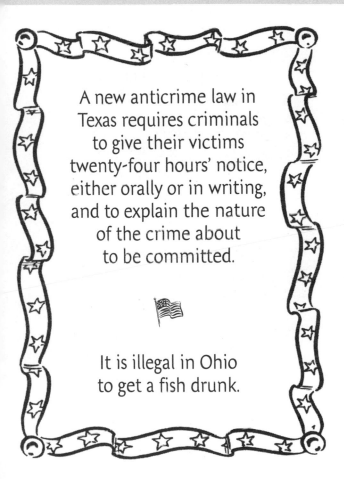

A new anticrime law in
Texas requires criminals
to give their victims
twenty-four hours' notice,
either orally or in writing,
and to explain the nature
of the crime about
to be committed.

It is illegal in Ohio
to get a fish drunk.

"I love sports.
Whenever I can,
I always watch the
Detroit Tigers on the radio."
—*Gerald Ford*

Surely paintings on velvet
couldn't have been dreamed
up anywhere else.

Home of the
All-You-Can-Eat buffet.

Thanks to Starbucks,
cappuccino *seems* American.

Watching the
Weather Channel
is so soothing!

"Vespucciland" wouldn't
have sounded as good.

The face of Lincoln on the penny
faces to the right, whereas the
face of all other presidents
on coins face to the left.

"The New Frontier of which I speak
is not a set of promises—it is a set
of challenges. It sums up not what
I intend to offer the American people,
but what I intend to ask of them."

—*John F. Kennedy, 1960*

Survivor shows
American can-do spirit.

There are more
plastic flamingos in
America than real ones.

Sleepaway camp in Maine.

The Pulitzer Prizes.

It's kind of cool the way Americans rejected the metric system.

Processed "American cheese" may not taste all that great to you, but it melts perfectly.

"800" numbers.

We have the world's
scariest roller-coasters.

Jell-O molds
have a certain
robust cheerfulness.

"By the time we
got to Woodstock,
we were half a
million strong . . ."

Commitment
ceremonies.

Free refills.

A trip to Disney World
is every American
child's birthright.

Only the most pretentious
Americans pursue sports like
foxhunting and polo.

And no American goes
anywhere near bullfighting.

The American Palate

TV dinners

Cheerios

Eggo waffles

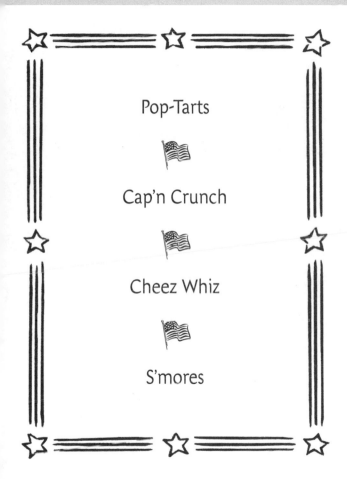

Pop-Tarts

Cap'n Crunch

Cheez Whiz

S'mores

Marshmallow Fluff

Good & Plenty

Juicy Fruit

Root beer

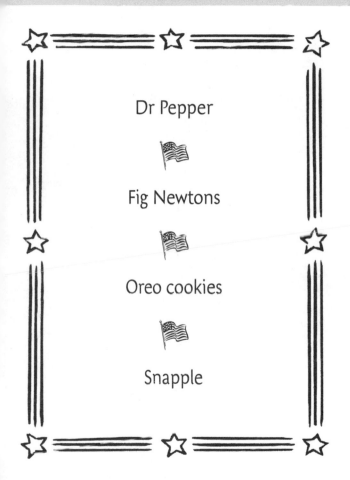

Dr Pepper

Fig Newtons

Oreo cookies

Snapple

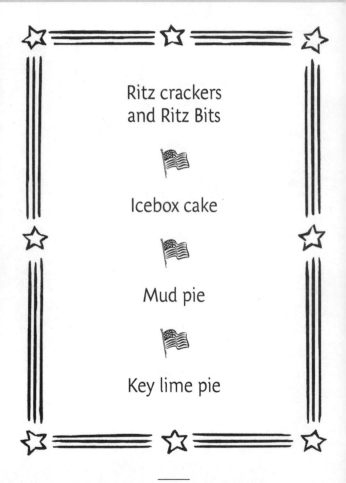

Ritz crackers
and Ritz Bits

Icebox cake

Mud pie

Key lime pie

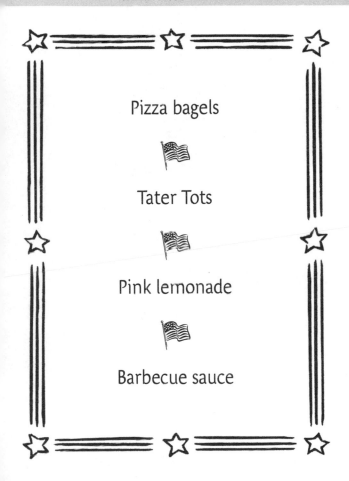

Pizza bagels

Tater Tots

Pink lemonade

Barbecue sauce

Corn dogs

Jiffy Pop popcorn

HoJo's fried clams

Fritos corn chips

Buffalo wings

Everyone, from all races, creeds,
and genders, is free to try to
get out of jury duty.

A pedicurist on every block.
(In New York City, anyway.)

Reading scores for kids
can't possibly get lower.

At least the guillotine
wasn't invented here.

When Americans hear
about a new healthy food,
they eat so much of
it that they get sick.

Mr. Potato Head has
been amusing/scaring
children for decades.

Hey—we're trying to make
public transportation work.

The California Raisin Board
did a good job with those
Claymation raisin guys.

"America is God's crucible, the great
melting pot where all the races of
Europe are melting and re-forming!"
—*Israel Zangwill, 1908*

There's nothing
an American reader
loves so much as a
good British mystery.

Coca-Cola makes a
great rust remover.

You can buy bales
of hay on-line!

The ladybug is the
official state bug
of Delaware.

"I think I did pretty well,
considering I started out
with nothing but a bunch
of blank paper."
—*Steve Martin*

The Peace Corps
was founded here.

There's nothing like a good
infomercial at two in the morning.

In some countries,
American gum and cigarettes
are better than money.

CNN.

We always had the best sneakers
in the world—and always will.

What Ms. Friedman's Third Grade Class Thinks Is so Great About America

FAO Schwarz.

We have the best pets.

It's very safe.

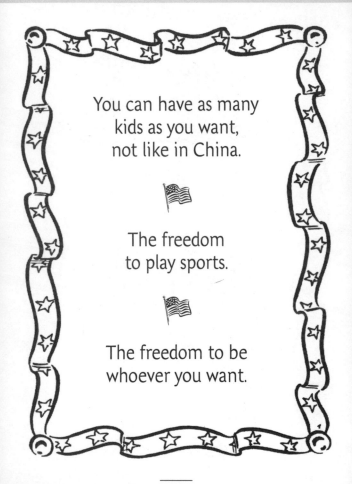

You can have as many
kids as you want,
not like in China.

The freedom
to play sports.

The freedom to be
whoever you want.

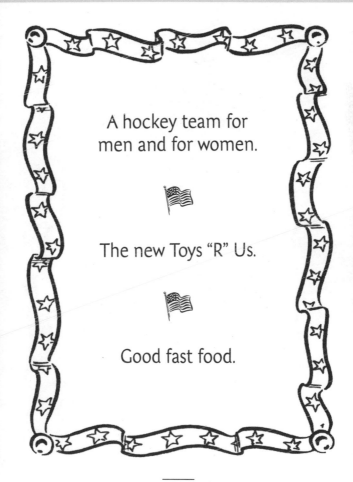

A hockey team for
men and for women.

The new Toys "R" Us.

Good fast food.

There's always
a place in America
to go on vacation.

We get to vote.

Great hands-on
museums.

Great sports leagues.

We're free to be messy.

Kids get lots of attention.

People protect you
from bad ideas.

The Marshall Plan
worked out very nicely.

The New World sounds shinier
than the Old World.

"Real liberty is neither found
in despotism or the extremes
of democracy, but in
moderate governments."
—*Alexander Hamilton*

Bluebirds are starting
to come back.

And the whooping crane
situation isn't entirely hopeless.

"From my tribe
I take nothing—
I am the maker
of my own fortune."

—*Tecumseh*

The official state gem of
Michigan is chlorastrolite.
(But wouldn't you rather
have a diamond?)

Ben & Jerry's
ice cream.

We already
speak English!

74

Miami Beach:
a little bit of South America,
without the hassle of
going through customs.

Coney Island.

Arizona has official
state neckwear: the bolo tie.

Driving
cross-country.

EZ Pass.

A survey of international
travel writers says America
has the best toilets
in the world.

The Miss America Pageant: Secrets of the Contestants

Be from a southern state.

Apply Vaseline to your teeth.

Don't forget to use two-sided tape on your bottom.

And duct tape on your breasts.

Try to be blonde.

"Talent portion" advice:
Perform the familiar
and hummable.

Don't even *think* about entering
without a personal consultant.

Martha's Vineyard.

Dick Clark and
his magical DNA.

Stop by the Price Club and pick up
a case of mustard, five gallons of
mouthwash, a thousand diapers,
and a pearl-and-diamond ring
for your sweetheart.

Band-Aid bandages with
pictures of Elmo and
Pokémon; shampoo bottles
with Disney character tops.

Domestic flights are easier to
book than international ones.

Oklahoma could never have
been written by a foreigner.

You can buy decent
tooth-bleaching kits
over the counter now.

Our lipstick copywriters
have come up with an
infinite number of
ways to say "red."

The fast-food industry never sleeps
in its efforts to siphon more fat
into the American public.

American Beauty roses.

There's something strangely
beautiful about a vast
parking lot filled with
yellow school buses.

"In America, there are two
classes of travel: first class,
and with children."
—*Robert Benchley*

America eats at least eighteen
acres of pizza a year.

The oldest living thing in the
world is the creosote bush
in California's Mojave Desert.
It is at least ten thousand years old.

In America, every citizen
has a right to sue.

According to legend,
George Washington donated
some of his own silver to
the mint to make coins.

Sneer if you want, but
getting married in Las Vegas
is a time-honored tradition.

The wider our TV screens
get, the wider *we* get.

Best Annual American Parties

The Golden Globes at the Beverly Hilton Hotel in Beverly Hills, California

Halloween at the University of Wisconsin, Madison

New Year's Eve
at Times Square

Marylou Whitney's
Saratoga ball

Mardi Gras
in New Orleans

The Grand Old Party

The Democratic Party

Hulaween, Bette Midler's
fundraiser for the New
York Restoration Project

Elizabeth Taylor's
next wedding

When we are tourists in
other countries, we really
stand out (okay, maybe
not always in a good way).

From the American Girl catalog:
"Introducing 'Kit Kittredge' . . . a clever,
resourceful girl growing up in 1934
during America's Great Depression. . . .
Kit comes to you dressed in a skirt and
twinset ensemble, along with sandals,
cotton underwear, and a barrette for
her thick blond hair." $84.00.

You haven't seen a flower
until you're seen one of Georgia
O'Keeffe's paintings of a flower.

It's great the way we have
rehabilitated funky old woebegone
train stations and turned them
into trendy food courts, isn't it?

The Rose Bowl Flea Market.

You can shop till you drop
at the Pittsburgh airport.

Also at Union Station
in Washington, D.C.

As long as your name is
Kelly, you can always find
a cute souvenir do-hickey
with your name on it at
any airport gift shop.

PBS, Disney, Nickelodeon:
the cheapest baby-sitters
you could ask for.

Did you know that
Eisenhower created NASA?

Or that John Denver suggested
the Civilian-in-Space program?

You don't have to go gray;
in the States we go blonde.

A lot of countries
sent over a lot of boats
trying to discover us.

"Can you please rephrase that
in the form of a question?"

Thank you, Merv Griffin,
for inventing *Jeopardy!*

Naturally, the smile button
was designed here.

Winslow Homer was
such a good painter
that his maritime scenes
make you feel wet.

We Allow Everyone a Second Chance

John McEnroe

John Travolta

Cher

Liddy Dole

Geraldo Rivera

Patty Hearst

Robert Downey Jr.

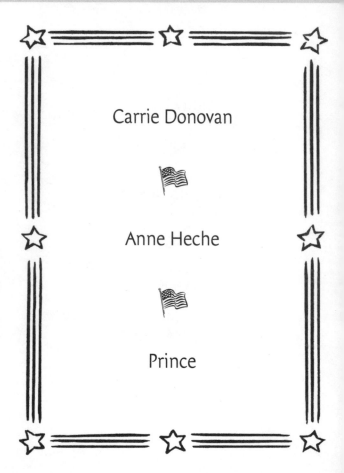

Carrie Donovan

Anne Heche

Prince

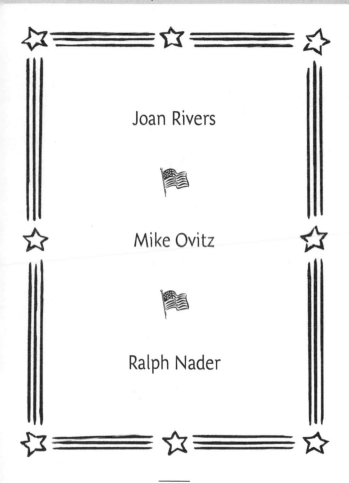

Joan Rivers

Mike Ovitz

Ralph Nader

O. J. Simpson

Greta Van Susteren

Sean Combs.
I mean Puff Daddy.
Oh, I forgot, it's P. Diddy.

The All-Star Game.

March Madness.

"Half of the American people
never read a newspaper.
Half never voted for president.
One hopes it is the same half."

—*Gore Vidal*

You can win the Best Supporting Actress Oscar one year, and not work again for years.

Where would the men of the world be without America's sun-kissed blondes?

"There never was a good war or a bad peace."
—*Benjamin Franklin*

Everyone can have a
kitchen drawer filled
with take-out menus.

We still care deeply about
Elvis and his family.

Whenever a book is
published about the
Kennedys, we will read it.

A thirty-two-ounce soda
is now considered
a single serving.

Open mike night.

Illumination Night in
Oak Bluffs, Massachusetts.

If it can be made in a
low-fat version, it will be.

In *McTeague* (1899), writer
Frank Norris used the term
"far out" to mean extreme
and imaginative.

"The income tax has made
more liars out of the American
people than golf has."
—*Will Rogers*

Flapper dresses
still look sexy.

We are not afraid to
steal the best of
European TV.
And the worst.

Edgar Allan Poe invented
the detective story.

Some of our goat cheeses
are just as good as
the French ones.

Some of our wines
are better.

Casual Fridays
were a nice innovation.

Great American Pastimes

Running under the sprinkler.

Toasting marshmallows.

Shopping at
Filene's Basement.

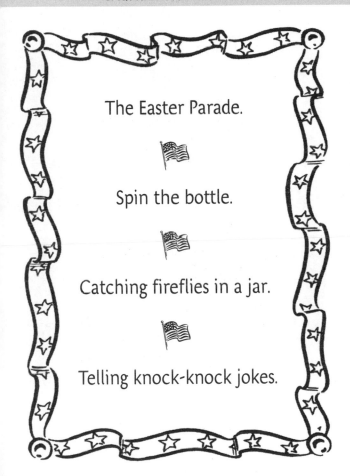

The Easter Parade.

Spin the bottle.

Catching fireflies in a jar.

Telling knock-knock jokes.

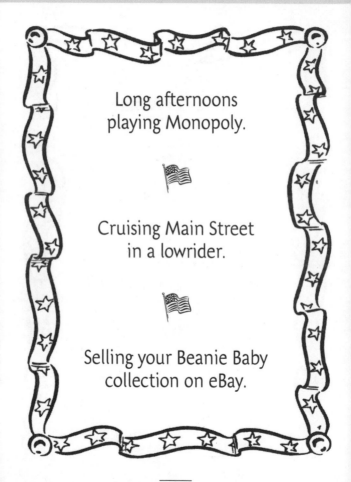

Long afternoons
playing Monopoly.

Cruising Main Street
in a lowrider.

Selling your Beanie Baby
collection on eBay.

Sandlot baseball,
whatever a "sandlot" is.

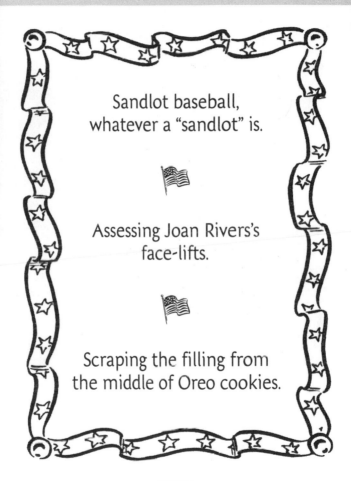

Assessing Joan Rivers's
face-lifts.

Scraping the filling from
the middle of Oreo cookies.

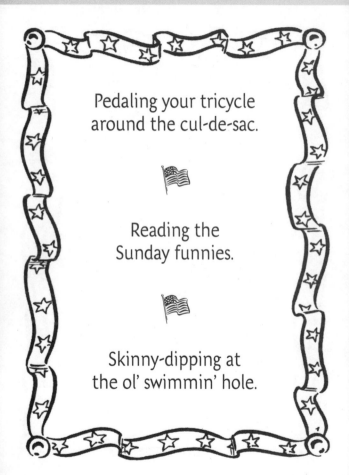

Pedaling your tricycle
around the cul-de-sac.

Reading the
Sunday funnies.

Skinny-dipping at
the ol' swimmin' hole.

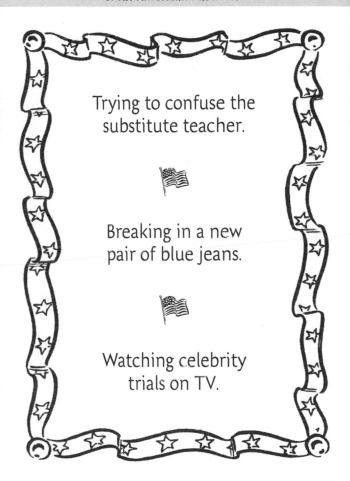

Trying to confuse the
substitute teacher.

Breaking in a new
pair of blue jeans.

Watching celebrity
trials on TV.

In Columbus, Ohio, there
is a replica of Seurat's
A Sunday on the Isle of Grande Jatte
made entirely of topiary.

Name one other
country where you get
Martin Luther King Day off.

Botox and laser peels
during lunchtime.

"Scrapbooking" has now become a verb, not to mention a popular course in adult education programs.

NBA stars build phenomenal compounds with sky-high ceilings. But then they have to sell them as part of their divorce or palimony settlements.

You can buy any size Scrabble now: large-tile, travel, magnetic, key-ring size, 3-D, and Deluxe with a rotating board.

Only in America . . .

Could there be fish-flavored
bottled water for cats.

Could a man like
Jerry Springer become
mayor of Cincinnati . . .

And then get his
own talk show.

Would Bantam Books
reprint Beatrix Potter's
books with illustrations
by a different artist.

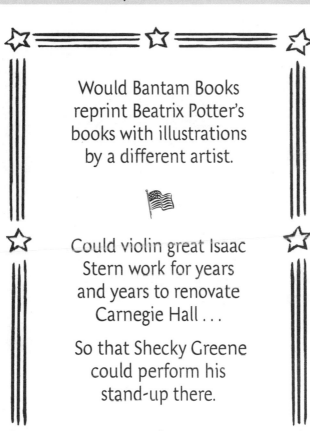

Could violin great Isaac
Stern work for years
and years to renovate
Carnegie Hall ...

So that Shecky Greene
could perform his
stand-up there.

Is it possible to hire a
tutor to help your toddler
get into preschool.

Could your hairdresser
get better seats than you
at the Knicks game.

Could Siegfried and Roy
become multimillionaires.

Could Arnold Schwarzenegger
become the highest paying
male actor, earning
$30 million a picture.

Could you hire someone
to babyproof your house.

Could you send your
dog to day care.

Will a scale tell you in
a loud, clear voice exactly
how much you weigh.

Would someone invent
sleeping bags for ferrets.

Would someone invent
battery-powered flour sifters.

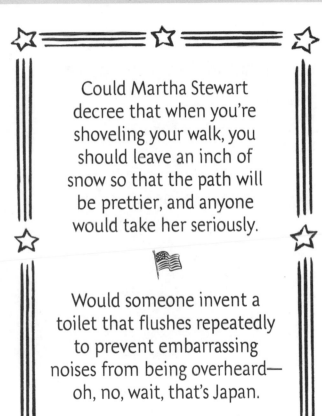

Could Martha Stewart
decree that when you're
shoveling your walk, you
should leave an inch of
snow so that the path will
be prettier, and anyone
would take her seriously.

Would someone invent a
toilet that flushes repeatedly
to prevent embarrassing
noises from being overheard—
oh, no, wait, that's Japan.

Americans love their nostalgia.

Noel Coward had to fill in for
Liberace in Las Vegas once.

FedEx.

Big Sur.

"It is no secret that organized crime in America takes in over forty billion dollars a year. This is quite a profitable sum, especially when one considers that the Mafia spend very little on office supplies."

—*Woody Allen*

Big breakfasts with pancakes and eggs and bacon and home fries.

Denim can be recycled . . .
and recycled.

We love talk shows so much that
we invented the all-talk network.

The eastern black walnut
is the official state
tree nut of Missouri.

"Rarely is the question asked:
Is our children learning?"
—*George W. Bush*

Our dental care is hands-
down the best in history.

Our kids have gotten slumber
parties down to a fine art.

Julia Child could only have been
born in the United States.

Large populations of
escaped, naturalized
parakeets live in Florida.

Every few years, America loses its
innocence in some kind of tragedy.
Then it finds it again.

Motown.

Self-adhesive postage
stamps are reason enough
to live here.

International House of Pancakes
is American.

Baseball was our idea.

"Americans always try to do
the right thing after they've
tried everything else."
—*Winston Churchill*

Christian County, Kentucky, is wet,
while Bourbon County is dry.
Barren County has the most
fertile land in the state.

Call us corrupt,
but don't call us dirty—
we take *a lot* of showers.

There are more public
libraries in this country
than McDonald's restaurants.

We created jazz, hepcat.

Down south, they put
peanuts in Coke.

Spiffy military uniforms.

Four time zones,
which is more than
you can say for France.

You can get a great deal
on a winter coat at a
Veterans Day sale.

Snowy Vermont towns are
picture-postcard perfect.

Drug stores sell just about
everything nowadays.

Saltwater taffy
on the boardwalk.

There's still some of
Alaska left unplundered.

Rochester, New York:
home of the white hotdogs.

Sunday Night Rituals

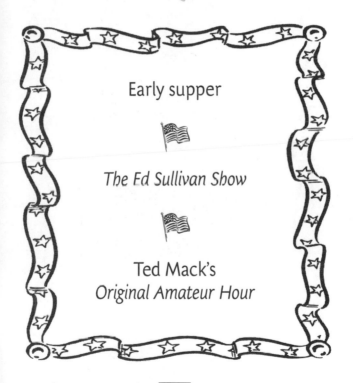

Early supper

The Ed Sullivan Show

Ted Mack's
Original Amateur Hour

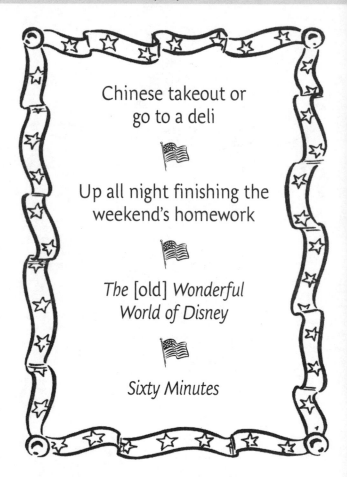

Chinese takeout or
go to a deli

Up all night finishing the
weekend's homework

The [old] *Wonderful
World of Disney*

Sixty Minutes

It's not called
"typing paper" anymore,
it's called "Xerox paper."

There is a generational
nobility in having been a
part of a failed dot-com.

Heinz makes purple
and green ketchup.

In this country,
people dedicate their
books to their cats . . .

And allow their dogs
to be the witnesses
at their weddings . . .

And leave their estates
to their pet birds.

You can't beat us when it
comes to loony new religions.

The United States had a
higher percentage of Y2K
nuts than any other nation.

There are now more white-
tailed deer in the United States
than there were when the
Mayflower landed.

The mouths of the presidents'
faces on Mount Rushmore
are eighteen feet high.

Amelia Earhart:
coolest woman in history.

No, wait—Janis Joplin:
coolest woman in history.

No, wait—Jacqueline Kennedy Onassis:
coolest woman in history.

No, wait . . .

Cool Real American Jobs

The person who cleans the faces at Mount Rushmore

The White House curator

The Rockettes' casting director

The Starbucks taste tester

The Stars and Stripes make
a great bikini pattern.

The United Nations is here
(okay, so we don't pay our dues).

"Wherever I have gone in this country,
I have found Americans."

—*Alf Landon (Republican candidate for
president who ran against FDR)*

American fashion designers can be just as expensive as European ones.

"Hollywood is a great place if you're an orange."

—*Fred Allen*

American painter Thomas Eakins studied in Europe for only four years, but his portraits have been compared to Rembrandt's.

President Taft was once
offered a contract to pitch
for the Cincinnati Reds.

Over 1,000 tornadoes touch down in
the United States every year—more
than in any other country in the world.

The longest tennis rally in
history took place in San Diego,
California, on February 5, 2000.
(15,674 hits, but who's counting?)

We saved the buffalo from extinction
(after almost killing them off).

Checks and balances was
a very good idea.

So was "of the people, by the
people, for the people."

Home of the world's
largest artichoke.

Only country to have a mascot
with the word "bald" in it.

Alphabetically speaking,
only superseded by Afghanistan,
Albania, and Algeria.

Birthplace of the dishwasher.

Younger than most European countries,
so there is less history to learn.

America is "the home of the brave," but
you don't have to be brave to live here.

To make them sound more appealing,
prunes were officially renamed
"dried plums" in 2000.

Girls aren't expected to work
on samplers anymore.

A varsity-letter sweater or jacket
never goes out of style.

President Andrew Johnson
was the only president who
sewed his own clothes.

Nobody Knows How to Name Towns Like We Do

Intercourse, Alabama

Unalaska, Alaska

Why, Arizona

Romance, Arkansas

Toadsuck, Arkansas

Frying Pan, California

Sucker Flat, California

Surprise, California

You Bet, California

Hygiene, Colorado

Howey-in-the-Hills, Florida

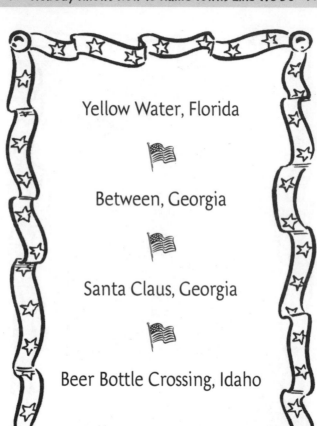

Yellow Water, Florida

Between, Georgia

Santa Claus, Georgia

Beer Bottle Crossing, Idaho

Roachtown, Illinois

Fickle, Indiana

Surprise, Indiana

Toad Hop, Indiana

What Cheer, Iowa

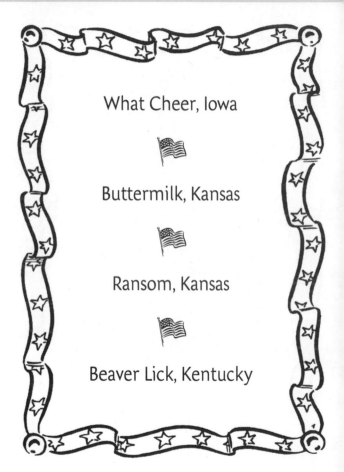

Buttermilk, Kansas

Ransom, Kansas

Beaver Lick, Kentucky

Monkey's Eyebrow,
Kentucky

Rabbit Hash, Kentucky

Eros, Louisiana

Fort Necessity, Louisiana

Uncle Sam, Louisiana

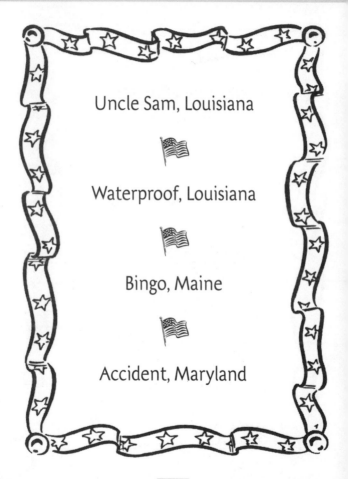

Waterproof, Louisiana

Bingo, Maine

Accident, Maryland

Assawoman, Maryland

Boring, Maryland

California, Maryland

Ware, Massachusetts
("I'm from Ware.")

Bad Axe, Michigan

Climax, Minnesota

Embarrass, Minnesota

Sleepy Eye, Minnesota

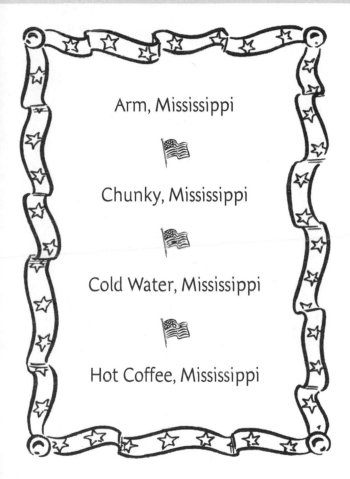

Arm, Mississippi

Chunky, Mississippi

Cold Water, Mississippi

Hot Coffee, Mississippi

Enough, Missouri

Romance, Missouri

Tightwad, Missouri

Useful, Missouri

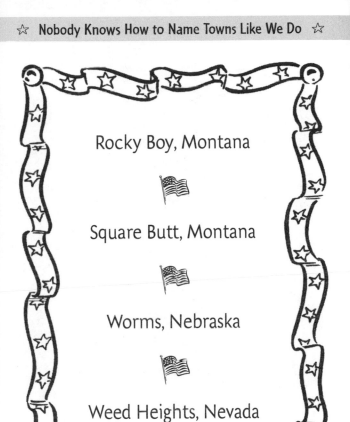

Rocky Boy, Montana

Square Butt, Montana

Worms, Nebraska

Weed Heights, Nevada

Hell Hollow,
New Hampshire

Lost Nation,
New Hampshire

Egg Harbor, New Jersey

Love Ladies, New Jersey

Elephant Butte,
New Mexico

Truth or Consequences,
New Mexico

Cat Elbow Corner,
New York

Hicksville, New York

Neversink, New York

Kill Devil Hills,
North Carolina

Meat Camp, North Carolina

Toast, North Carolina

Concrete, North Dakota

Blue Ball, Ohio

Three Legs Town, Ohio

Cookie Town, Oklahoma

Pumpkin Center, Oklahoma

Slaughterville, Oklahoma

Idiotville, Oregon

Half.com, Oregon

Bath Addition, Pennsylvania

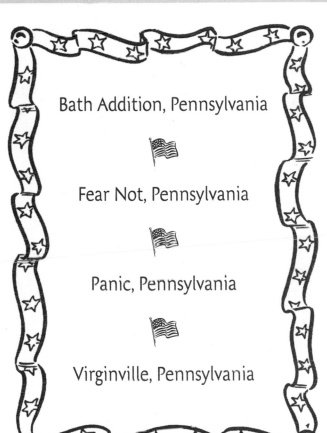

Fear Not, Pennsylvania

Panic, Pennsylvania

Virginville, Pennsylvania

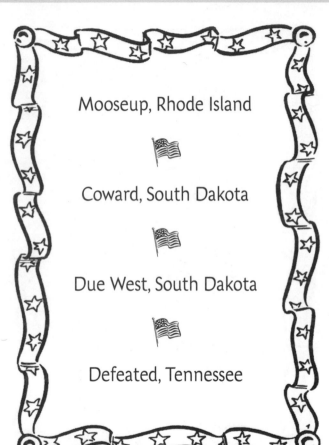

Mooseup, Rhode Island

Coward, South Dakota

Due West, South Dakota

Defeated, Tennessee

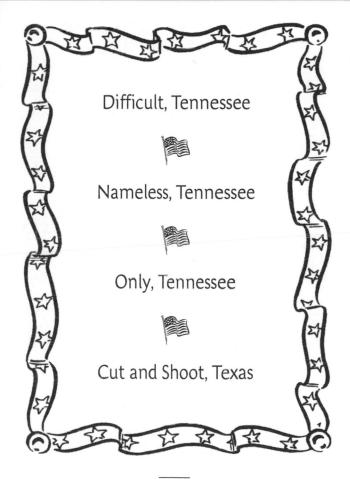

Difficult, Tennessee

Nameless, Tennessee

Only, Tennessee

Cut and Shoot, Texas

Ding Dong, Texas

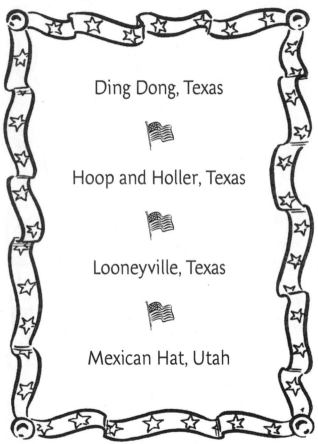

Hoop and Holler, Texas

Looneyville, Texas

Mexican Hat, Utah

Satan's Kingdom,
Vermont

Fourway, Virginia
(two of them)

Walla Walla,
Washington

Big Ugly, West Virginia

War, West Virginia

Imalone, Wisconsin

Muddy Gap, Wyoming

President Lyndon Johnson was
so concerned with secrecy that he
often wrote "Burn This" on letters.

"Football features two of the worst
aspects of American life—violence
and committee meetings."
—*George Will*

There have been four different
U.S. postage stamps
commemorating Canadians.

Mary Cassatt was the only
American to exhibit with
the French Impressionists.

"America did not invent human
rights. In a very real sense . . .
human rights invented America."
—*Jimmy Carter*

We brought instant
replay to sports coverage.

Native American moccasins
were the original Tod's shoe.

"I was recently on a tour of
Latin America, and the only regret
I have is that I didn't study my
Latin harder in school so I could
converse with those people."
—*Dan Quayle*

American grown-ups aren't
ashamed to wear braces.

We have the hardest
to sing national anthem.

Harriet Beecher Stowe's
Uncle Tom's Cabin was one of the
main catalysts of the Civil War.

We didn't come up with the idea
for Valentine's Day, but we sure
commercialized the heck out of it.

Lewis and Clark
were excellent campers.

Guess we proved
Karl Marx wrong.

"Every morning I get up and
look through the *Forbes* lists of
the richest people in America.
If I'm not there, I go to work."

—*Robert Orben*

Cigarette commercials
are banned from TV.

There's a chance you might be able
to interest your children in colonial
history if you visit Williamsburg.

If not, you'll at least get
good ideas for colors to paint
the walls in your house.

"Californians are a race of people; they are not merely inhabitants of a state."
—O. Henry

Ben Franklin invented electricity, or whatever was he doing with that kite?

The opossum is America's only native marsupial.

On the winning side
of both world wars.

During President Reagan's tenure,
the White House bought
twelve tons of jelly beans.

Streaking was kind of fun.
To watch, anyway.

Make Your Own Tang

1 tb. sugar

½ tb. fructose

¼ tsp. citric acid

⅓ of ⅛ tsp. calcium phosphate

Potassium citrate

¾ tsp. orange extract or orange juice solids

¼ of ⅛ tsp. ascorbic acid (vitamin C)

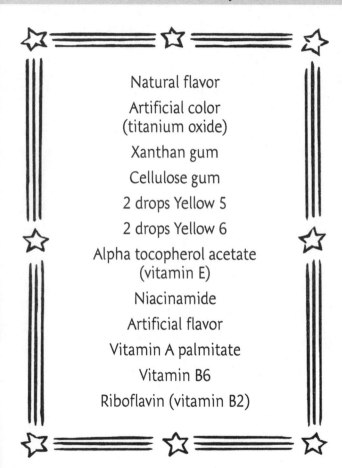

Natural flavor

Artificial color
(titanium oxide)

Xanthan gum

Cellulose gum

2 drops Yellow 5

2 drops Yellow 6

Alpha tocopherol acetate
(vitamin E)

Niacinamide

Artificial flavor

Vitamin A palmitate

Vitamin B6

Riboflavin (vitamin B2)

"The chief business of the
American people is business."
—*President Calvin Coolidge*

Anyone can become president . . .
even Millard Fillmore.

Our fall colors are the
best and the brightest.

Okay, so we don't have *the* Eiffel Tower.
But we do have a replica in Las Vegas
that rises fifty stories above a
hotel and casino complex.

It's right near Venice
and Ancient Egypt.

If you're lucky, Goodwill
will pick up your old stuff for you.

"I love America more than any other country in this world, and exactly for this reason: I insist on the right to criticize her perpetually."

—*James Baldwin*

Labor Day:
How else do you know when to put away your summer clothes?

Horatio Alger.

Quaker Oatmeal.

Warm apple pie
with a slice of
cheddar cheese.

Presidents' Day weekend.

It's called *USA Today*.

They are penny loafers,
not Krugerrand loafers.

The Spirit of St. Louis.

"In the United States there is
more space where nobody is
than where anybody is. This is
what makes America what it is."
—*Gertrude Stein*

Panty hose was invented here.

Something important
happened in 1812, right?

You can find good
tourmaline in Maine.

And some beautiful
turquoise in New Mexico.

Toll House cookies were invented when a woman chopped a slab of chocolate into bits, thinking the chocolate would melt evenly throughout the batter.

The Statue of Liberty is even more impressive in person.

Those cute little Campbell's twins.

And Buster Brown.

It's kind of fun to memorize
the state capitals.

"This is the Fourth?"
—*Thomas Jefferson's last words*

Mattel changed Barbie's
measurements to make her
more realistic, but she's
still pretty stacked.

Male action figures, meanwhile,
are as fantastically buff as ever.

The Little Lord Fauntleroy look
still has a foothold among American
mothers of a certain type.

People used to think that
watermelons caused fevers,
but not anymore.

The official muffin of New York
is the apple muffin.

There would never have been
malt shops without us.

"A gentleman will not insult me,
and no man not a gentleman
can insult me."

—*Frederick Douglass*

It's cute the way women
watch the Super Bowl
for the commercials.

Feel free to eat on the street
here—everyone else does.

It's impossible to
buy sheets *not* on sale
at Bloomingdale's.

Teen pregnancies are down.

Americans have the right to bear arms, even though no one can agree on what this actually means.

"Leave the matter of religion to the family altar, the church, and the private school, supported entirely by private contributions. Keep the church and the state forever separate."

—*Ulysses S. Grant, 1875*

Navajo rugs make
any room look terrific.

How about
that Tupperware?

You don't have to get
dressed up for a clambake.

We Take Credit for All Talented Canadians

Mike Myers; Joni Mitchell,
Neil Young, Gordon Lightfoot,
John Candy, Dan Aykroyd,
Paul Shaffer, Lorne Michaels,
Martin Short, Eugene Levy,
Andrea Martin, Rick Moranis,
Michael J. Fox, k. d. lang.

For some reason
we don't take credit
for Celine Dion, however.

A two-ocean country.

Basketball was born in
Springfield, Massachusetts, in 1891,
and now everyone plays it—
well, 250 million worldwide.

Americans spend more than
three times as much on salty snacks
as they do on public libraries.

Way to go,
Miracle at Lake Placid!

Chris and Dana Reeve.

"900 Trillion Bajillion Served."

Great American Clowns

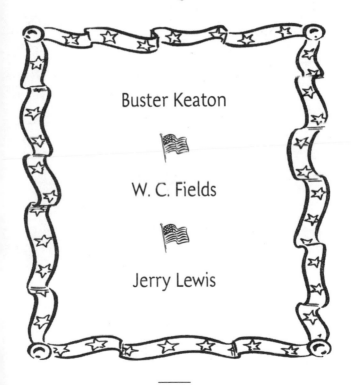

Buster Keaton

W. C. Fields

Jerry Lewis

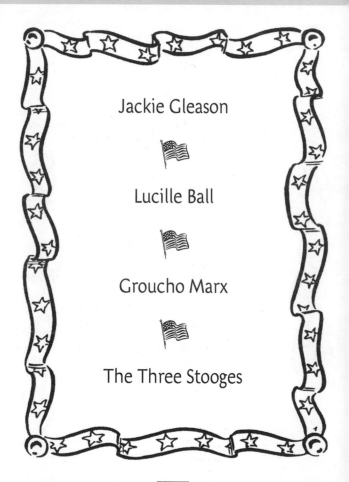

Jackie Gleason

Lucille Ball

Groucho Marx

The Three Stooges

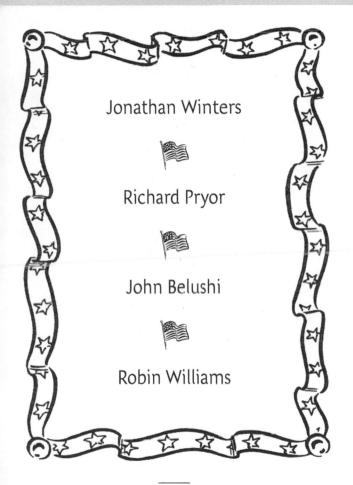

Jonathan Winters

Richard Pryor

John Belushi

Robin Williams

Scharffen Berger chocolate
can compete with the
finest imports.

Connecticut is currently
being plagued by an
overabundance of
cute, cute ladybugs.

We paid Russia two cents
an acre for Alaska.

American mothers welcome
newborn daughters just as
much as newborn sons.

Marie is a little bit country,
whereas Donny is a little
bit rock 'n' roll.

"Where seldom is heard
a discouraging word, and the
skies are not cloudy all day."

Every state has its
own bird and flower.

You can still buy underarm
dress shields and horehound
drops from the Vermont
Country Store catalog.

Michael Jackson
and Elizabeth Taylor
are such a cute couple.

American cocker spaniels
are less sprawly looking
than English cocker spaniels.

Not everyone would
appreciate the Everglades
the way we do.

Or the La Brea tar pits.

You're always welcome
at Our Lady of Peace's
annual roast-beef dinner.

The *New Yorker* magazine.

No one at Burger King will look
at you funny if you order
a Whopper with Cheese
without the meat.

The Cat in the Hat
revolutionized
children's books.

"Every American ought to
have the right to be treated
as he would wish to be treated,
as one would wish his
children to be treated.
This is not the case."

—*John F. Kennedy, 1960*

The world's most frequently
sung song (outside of national
anthems) was written by two
sisters from Louisville, Kentucky:
Mildred and Patricia Hill wrote
"Happy Birthday to You."

In 1825, John Quincy Adams
was the first U.S. president
to take the inaugural oath
wearing long pants.

"This American system of
ours, call it Americanism,
call it capitalism, call it what
you will, gives each and every
one of us a great opportunity
if we only seize it with both
hands and make the most of it."

—*Al Capone*

The Second City
comedy troupe.

The comfort of knowing that, no matter what, a Daley will be in power in Chicago.

You can buy figurines of Jesus playing hockey and Santa kneeling in front of the manger.

We proudly elect people like Jesse Ventura to high office.

Tomatoes came from
the New World.

So did tobacco.

Divorce ceremonies and
divorce parties are catching on.

Coyotes have made their
way all across the land.

"If I were asked . . . to what the singular prosperity and growing strength of [the Americans] ought mainly to be attributed, I should reply: to the superiority of their women."

—*Alexis de Tocqueville*

The Vietnam Memorial was designed by a college student.

World's fourth largest country
(after Russia, China, and Canada).

Everyone in the world
wants to vacation in Hawaii.

The Alaskan flag was designed
by a schoolchild.

"[Arizona] is my land, my home, my father's land, to which I now ask to be allowed to return. I want to spend my last days there, and be buried among those mountains. If this could be, I might die in peace."

—*Geronimo*

Our ornithologists will not give up the search for the ivory-billed woodpecker (last spotted fifty years ago).

"Good planners, people from New Jersey, Tepper thought, except for the plan they must have hatched at some point to move to New Jersey."

—*Calvin Trillin*

Fanny Farmer was the first cookbook author to insist on standardized measurements in every recipe.

Rubber flip-flops.

American flag motif sweaters.

Everyone of a certain age has a favorite photo from *Life* magazine.

Everyone of a certain age learned anatomy from *National Geographic*.

We Make the Best Sandwiches in the World

Peanut butter and jelly

Tunafish salad

BLT

Grilled American cheese

Turkey club

Hamburger

Cheeseburger

Chili dog
(It *is* a sandwich, when
you think about it.)

Hoagie

Philadelphia cheese steak

Po' boy

French dip

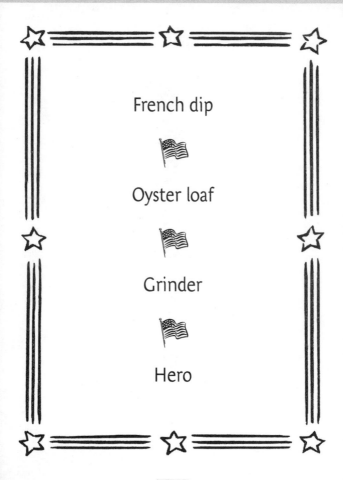

Oyster loaf

Grinder

Hero

"One does not sell the
land people walk on."
—*Chief Crazy Horse*

Pet psychiatrists.

Fewer nudist beaches than
in Europe . . . although, is this
a great or a not-great thing?

The rest of the world's
popular culture would
be nowhere without
the United States.

Not to mention
their T-shirts.

We like to think
our highway system
is the best in the world.

Michael Jordan is
instantly recognizable
in every country on Earth.

So is Muhammad Ali.

So is the Nike *swoosh*.

"After all, tomorrow is another day."

American women got
the vote in 1919—years
before the British women.

We do respect our Halloween.

We've been watching
George Clooney since
The Facts of Life.

When you reach the age where you want good, clean entertainment, say hello to Branson, Missouri.

Amtrak has a "quiet car" where cell phone conversations are prohibited.

Cheap gas!

Best cured beef in the world,
says the *New York Times*.

President Lincoln thought
his Gettysburg Address
was a "flat failure."

President Herbert Hoover began
each day at the White House
with a 7:30 game of medicine
ball, which was like volleyball.

Most of our money is kind of boring,
but those state quarters were
really a great idea.

"Fame is like a shaved pig with a
greased tail, and it is only after it
has slipped through the hands of
thousands, that some fellow, by
mere chance, holds onto it!"
—*Davy Crockett*

How 'bout those Mets?

Pussy willows only grow in
the United States, right?

A bird feeder outside
every kitchen window.

Dentists who distract their
patients by showing movies and
offering spa treatments.

Great American Slogans

Wonder Bread helps build
strong bodies twelve ways.

It's the real thing.

Come alive! You're in the
Pepsi Generation.

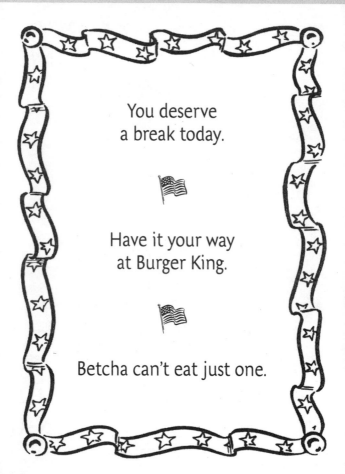

You deserve
a break today.

Have it your way
at Burger King.

Betcha can't eat just one.

If I have only one life to live,
let me live it as a blonde.

Does she or doesn't she?
Only her hairdresser
knows for sure.

Which twin has the Toni?

Wisk around
the collar beats
ring-around-the-collar.

Reach out and
touch someone.

It's not nice to fool
Mother Nature.

I can't believe
it's not butter!

Takes a licking and
keeps on ticking.

They're baked by little elves
in a hollow tree. . . .

Just a silly
millimeter longer.

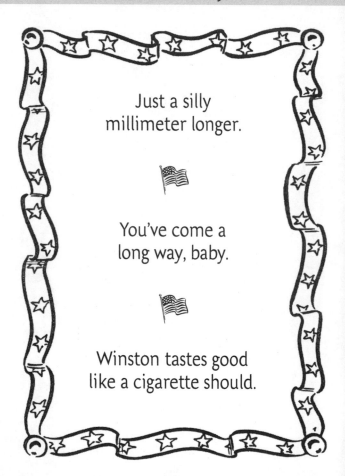

You've come a
long way, baby.

Winston tastes good
like a cigarette should.

In the valley of the
Jolly (ho-ho-ho)
Green Giant . . .

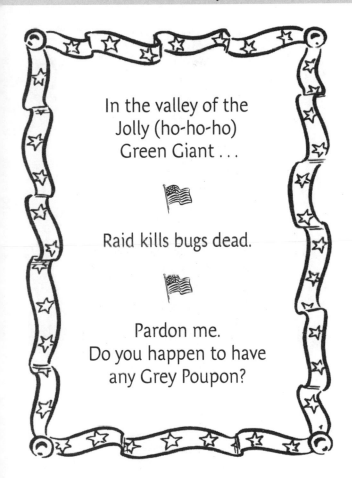

Raid kills bugs dead.

Pardon me.
Do you happen to have
any Grey Poupon?

Oh, I wish I were an
Oscar Mayer wiener . . .

Hot dogs!
Armour hot dogs!
What kind of kids eat
Armour hot dogs?

We try harder.

Where's the beef?

Mmm! Mmm! Good!

Charlie, Starkist don't
want tuna with good
taste. They want tuna
that tastes good.

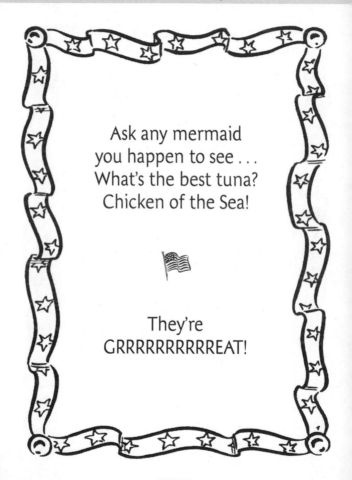

Ask any mermaid
you happen to see . . .
What's the best tuna?
Chicken of the Sea!

They're
GRRRRRRRRREAT!

Ding-dong!
Avon calling!

Plop-plop, fizz fizz,
Oh, what a relief it is!

Be all that you can be.

Breakfast of champions.

Bring out the Hellman's
and bring out the best.

Please don't squeeze
the Charmin.

A diamond
is forever.

A little dab'll do ya.

Look Ma,
no cavities!

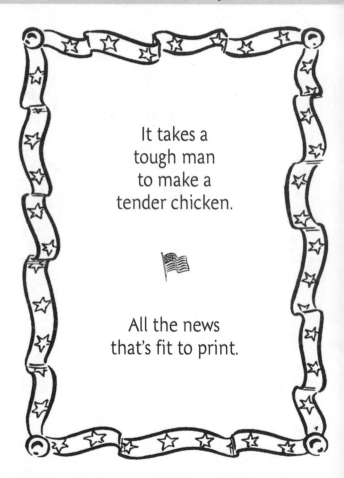

It takes a
tough man
to make a
tender chicken.

All the news
that's fit to print.

A mind is a terrible
thing to waste.

Don't leave home
without it.

Double your pleasure,
double your fun.

It's nice the way we
name candy bars after
our baseball players.

In case you were wondering:
When a flag is so worn it is
no longer fit to serve as a
symbol of our country,
it should be destroyed by
burning in a dignified manner.

Colonial America
is just so quaint.

Nothing like taking
an early morning run
by the reservoir.

Western-style
horseback riding.

241

We all respected Dolly Parton
for starting Dollywood.

What a great idea
those sandwich sliced
dill pickles were.

How much do we love
our wraps and smoothies?

Cape Cod potato chips—
a crispy bite of heaven.

Americans drive on the
right side of the road—
in more than one sense.

We didn't invent Lego toys,
but we sure took them seriously.

Dolly Madison
popularized ice cream.

Häagen-Dazs
perfected ice cream.
(Don't let the spelling fool
you; it's American, too.)

It's remarkable that a rest stop
on the New Jersey Turnpike
was named for Joyce Kilmer,
the poet who wrote,
"I think that I shall never see
A poem lovely as a tree."

Once you've ordered sea
monkeys from the back
of a comic book, you'll
never trust advertising again.

What a country:
a fake Prada or Fendi
bag for everyone!

If you know where to look,
you can probably find a bottle
of Woodward's Gripe Water
for your infant's tummy.

Even our big-city newspapers
give the time of the
sunrise and the sunset.

Cool Slang Words Through the Years

Giggle water,
hooch = alcohol

To be soaked with a
bar rag = to be tipsy

Barreled, bolognied, canned, pie-eyed, shellacked, spifficated, stewed to the hat = drunk

To lap = to drink alcohol

Nonskid = someone who can't hold her liquor

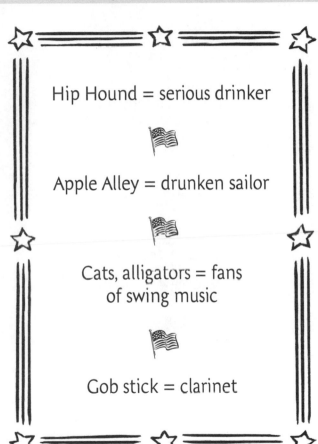

Hip Hound = serious drinker

Apple Alley = drunken sailor

Cats, alligators = fans
of swing music

Gob stick = clarinet

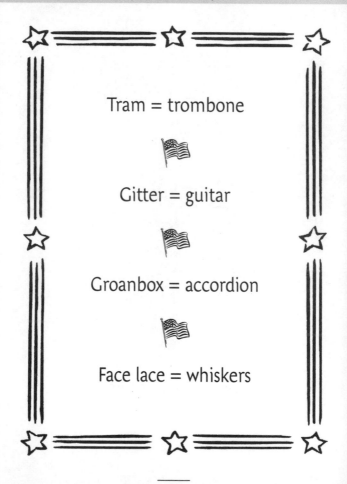

Tram = trombone

Gitter = guitar

Groanbox = accordion

Face lace = whiskers

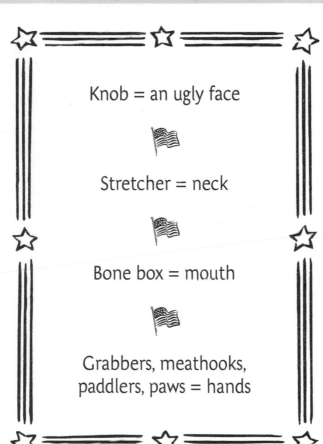

Knob = an ugly face

Stretcher = neck

Bone box = mouth

Grabbers, meathooks,
paddlers, paws = hands

Feelers, fish hooks, forks,
hooks, pickers, stealers
wigglers = fingers

Drumsticks, pillars,
stems, splits, uprights,
stumps = legs

Prayer dukes = knees

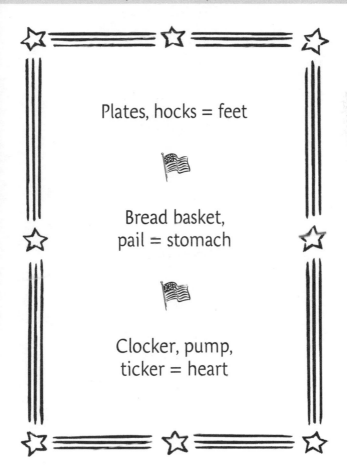

Plates, hocks = feet

Bread basket,
pail = stomach

Clocker, pump,
ticker = heart

A bear in the air = a police
officer in a helicopter

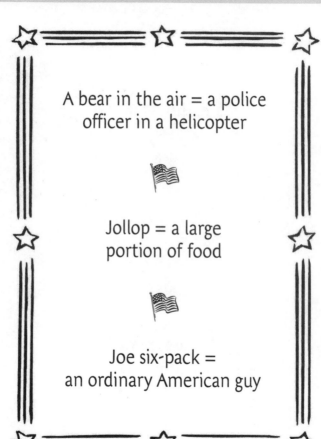

Jollop = a large
portion of food

Joe six-pack =
an ordinary American guy

Cat = guy

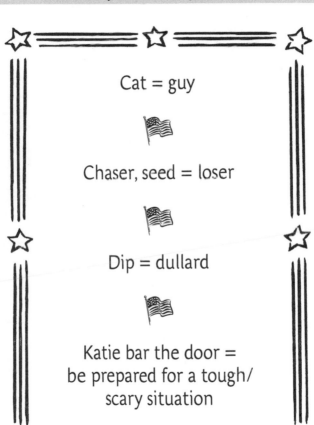

Chaser, seed = loser

Dip = dullard

Katie bar the door =
be prepared for a tough/
scary situation

Puzzle palace =
1) Army headquarters,
the Pentagon 2) a place like
the White House, where
important decisions are made

Eastern Western = a Chinese
or Japanese western-type of
movie, filled with violence
and macho behavior

KISS = keep it simple, stupid

Rusty-dusty = the buttocks

Cool whip = something
new and pleasant

Doy-burger = a dim-witted
or uncoordinated person

Bat cave = place to sleep

Tang out = to quit

Mommy up = to console, to hug, love

Ammunition = toilet paper

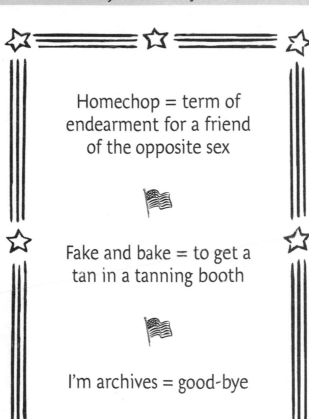

Homechop = term of endearment for a friend of the opposite sex

Fake and bake = to get a tan in a tanning booth

I'm archives = good-bye

Waitresses have
the best slang.

No, carnival barkers
have the best slang.

Whatever it is,
your next-door neighbor
has a better one.

The selflessness of our police
officers, our firefighters,
our rescue workers, and
our countless volunteers.

Children's birthday parties no
longer need to be held at home.

A long history of entertainment,
starting with the Boston Tea Party.

"No taxation without representation"— one of America's first great rhymes.

"Miss Mary Mack."

"Mairzy Doats and Dozy Doats."

Okay, so maybe the robber barons didn't always play fair, but they sure were rich.

Come to think of it, the Robber Barons would be a good name for a rock group.

Did anyone do as much for ducks as John James Audubon?

Jackson Pollock showed
the world that sometimes
a little spilling is okay.

Nobody's paintings can make
you feel as lonely and depressed
as Edward Hopper's.

Every American president with
a beard has been Republican.

We're very easy to
find on a globe.

We never run into the ocean
without remembering *Jaws*.

If it's true that Walt Disney
had his body frozen,
that's kind of interesting.

———

265

Ditto for Timothy Leary.

We pay our professional athletes
well. . . . Insanely well.

Dr. Spock revolutionized
parenting even before the
word "parenting" was coined.

French toast is American.

So are French fries.

Ditto English muffins.

Ditto Spanish omelettes.

"What the people want is very simple. They want an America as good as its promise."

—*Congresswoman Barbara Jordan*

"Give me health and a day
and I will make the pomp
of emperors ridiculous."
—*Ralph Waldo Emerson*

Picking berries on a
cool summer morning.

There is now an association
for eating-contest contestants.

"Remember the Alamo!"
—*Colonel Sidney Sherman*

"Hello Muddah, Hello Faddah"
—*Alan Sherman*

Herman Melville didn't realize
Moby-Dick was allegorical
until a reader told him so.

Starlings were imported here
by a man who wanted every bird
mentioned in Shakespeare to be
found in the United States.

George Washington slept here.

So did Wilt Chamberlain.

We're very fond of
our comfortable shoes.

The great Man O'War won all
of his horse races except one,
which he lost to a horse named Upset.

It took a long time, but
Nutella is finally catching on here.

Famous Writers from Almost Every State

Alabama: Harper Lee

Alaska:
Margaret Elizabeth Bell

Arizona: Linda Ronstadt

Arkansas: John Grisham

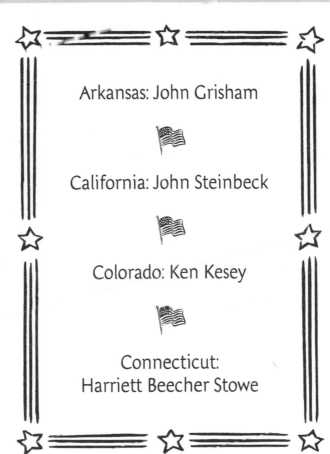

California: John Steinbeck

Colorado: Ken Kesey

Connecticut:
Harriett Beecher Stowe

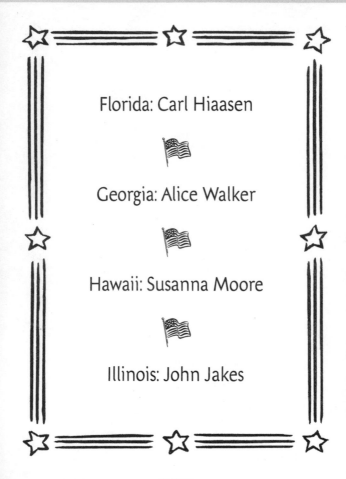

Florida: Carl Hiaasen

Georgia: Alice Walker

Hawaii: Susanna Moore

Illinois: John Jakes

Indiana: Theodore Dreiser

Iowa: Bess Street Aldrich

Kansas: William Inge

Kentucky: Bobbie Ann Mason

Louisiana: Truman Capote

Maine: Stephen King

Maryland: H. L. Mencken

Massachusetts:
Emily Dickinson

Michigan: Edna Ferber

Minnesota: F. Scott Fitzgerald

Mississippi: William Faulkner

Missouri:
William Least Heat Moon

Montana: Dorothy Baker

Nebraska: Mari Sandoz

Nevada:
Sarah Hopkins Winnemucca

New Hampshire: John Irving

New Jersey: Philip Roth

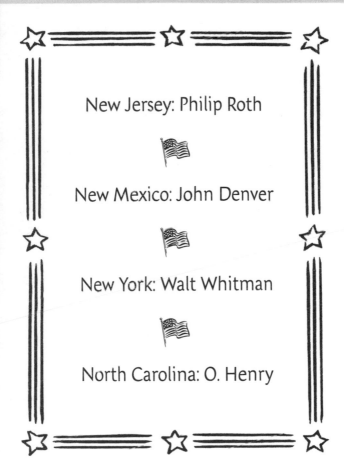

New Mexico: John Denver

New York: Walt Whitman

North Carolina: O. Henry

North Dakota: Louis L'Amour

Ohio: Clarence Page

Oklahoma: Garth Brooks

Oregon: Raymond Carver

Pennsylvania:
Maxwell Anderson

Rhode Island: H. P. Lovecraft

South Carolina:
Dubose Heyward

South Dakota: Tom Brokaw

Tennessee: Nikki Giovanni

Texas: Willie Nelson

Utah: Bernard De Voto

Vermont: Gail Sheehy

Virginia: William Styron

Washington: Lynda Barry

West Virginia:
Jayne Anne Phillips

Wisconsin: Peter Straub

*69.

Call waiting and the
liberty to disable it.

Wish I'd designed the
original bandana print.

The Empire State Building
when it's bathed in red,
white, and blue at night.

Call her what you will,
but Tammy Faye Bakker
is an American icon.

The Narragansett Bay
at sunset.

The Napa Valley gourmet
groceries have cornered
the market on cute and
tastefully expensive.

Kenneth Cole's provocative ads.

Each new gourmet water on the market makes you even smarter.

After the crash of 1929, we changed the rules so that can never happen again . . . didn't we?

The Chicago skyline.

Great Chicago Inventions

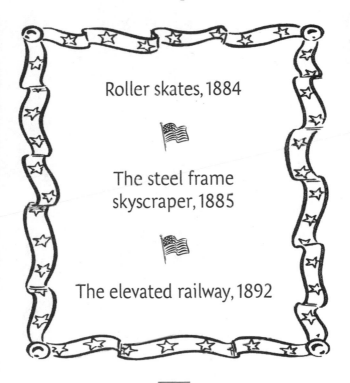

Roller skates, 1884

The steel frame skyscraper, 1885

The elevated railway, 1892

Cracker Jacks, 1893

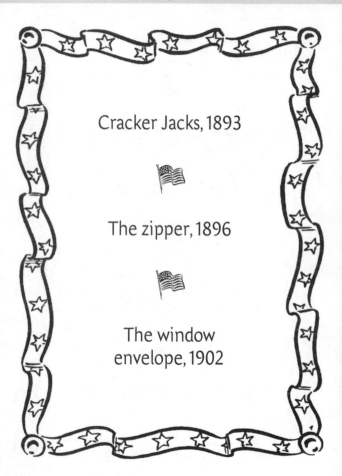

The zipper, 1896

The window
envelope, 1902

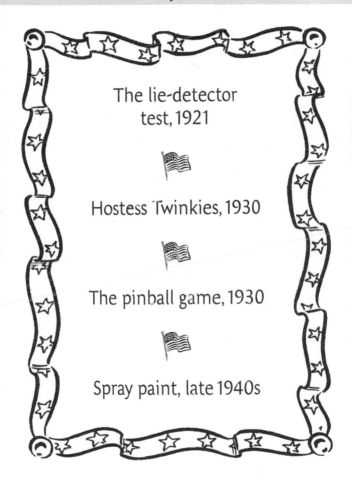

The lie-detector
test, 1921

Hostess Twinkies, 1930

The pinball game, 1930

Spray paint, late 1940s

Tolerance.

In much of the country, not only won't your classmates care if your parents are divorced, they won't care if your parents are married, never did marry, are of the same sex, or are a great single mom and a turkey baster.

Two words: day spa.

We import exotic fruit from all over the world, then mix it all up into a compote with our apples, grapes, and oranges.

Most schoolchildren will eventually learn their state's motto. (Many will then forget it.)

Think of all the time we save by not putting a "u" in words like labor, favor, and color.

We don't have our own tartans,
but we are careful about picking
out just the right bumper sticker.

Thank you, Paul Revere.

We are so resilient, we barely
remember how sad we were
when *L.A. Law* went off the air.

Edith Wharton.

We take our trends
so seriously.
Hello, yoga class.

Austin, Texas.

Great American Toys

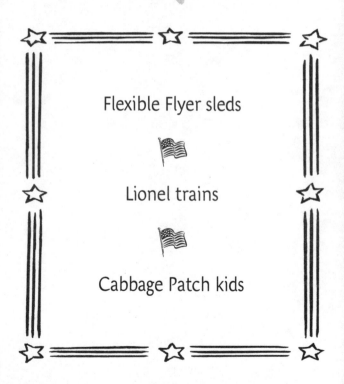

Flexible Flyer sleds

Lionel trains

Cabbage Patch kids

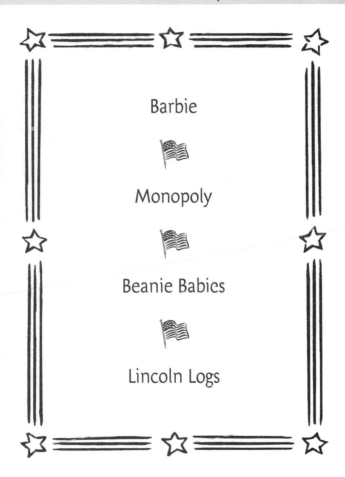

Barbie

Monopoly

Beanie Babies

Lincoln Logs

The Detroit Grand Prix—people
win big purses to do what's
ordinarily against the law.

The Little 500 at the
University of Indiana
at Bloomington.

We are the world's leading
exporter of junk food.

If we didn't already
have Las Vegas, we'd
have had to invent it.
Thank you, Bugsy Siegel.

Montana:
Looks just like Switzerland,
but without the euros or
the fancy accents.

We still have hippies all
over the place—from
San Francisco to Cape Cod,
from Key West to
Portland, Maine.

The town of Modesto, California,
was named after its founders,
who were too modest to name
a town after themselves.

Fields of daisies
and sunflowers.

"Goodnight, Mrs. Calabash,
wherever you are."
—*Jimmy Durante*

Americans know
how to pull together.

Real patriotism.

"God bless America,
my home sweet home."